All About Dogs

Shiba Inu

Katie Gillespie

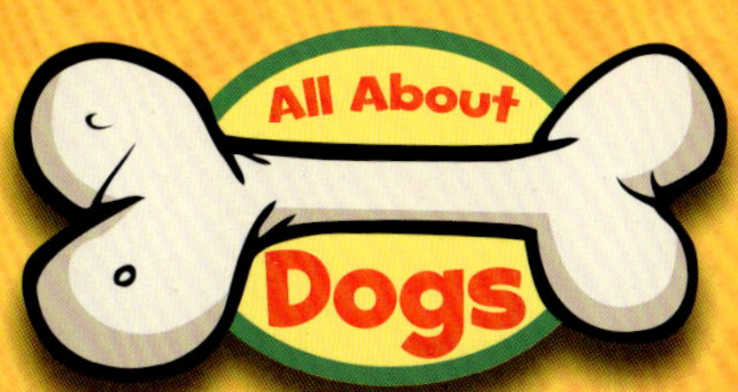

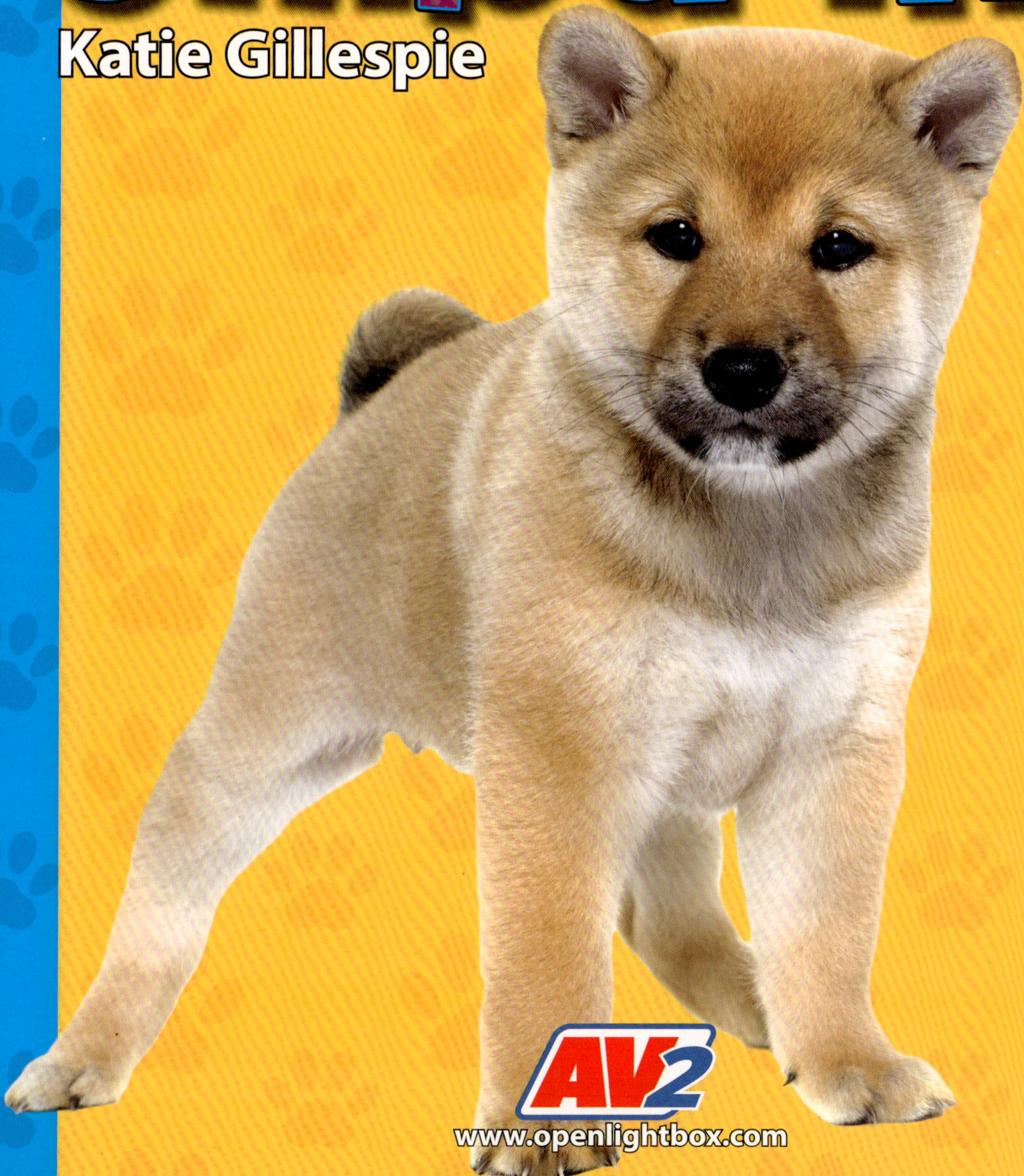

AV2
www.openlightbox.com

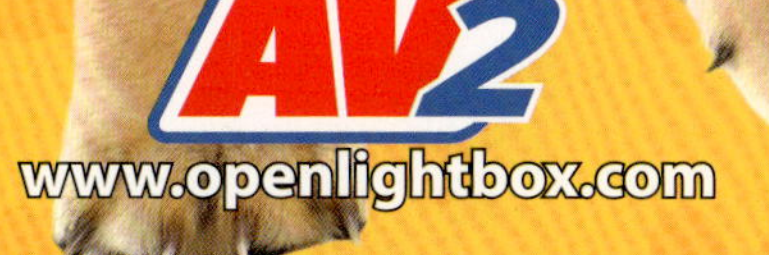

Step 1
Go to **www.openlightbox.com**

Step 2
Enter this unique code

BWJAPJS4H

Step 3
Explore your interactive eBook!

AV2 is optimized for use on any device

Your interactive eBook comes with...

Contents
Browse a live contents page to easily navigate through resources

Audio
Listen to sections of the book read aloud

Videos
Watch informative video clips

Weblinks
Gain additional information for research

Slideshows
View images and captions

Try This!
Complete activities and hands-on experiments

Key Words
Study vocabulary, and complete a matching word activity

Quizzes
Test your knowledge

Share
Share titles within your Learning Management System (LMS) or Library Circulation System

Citation
Create bibliographical references following the Chicago Manual of Style

This title is part of our AV2 digital subscription

1-Year K–5 Subscription
ISBN 978-1-7911-3320-7

Access hundreds of AV2 titles with our digital subscription.
Sign up for a FREE trial at **www.openlightbox.com/trial**

Contents

Name That Dog

Which active dog loves to go for walks?

Which dog is said to look like a fox?

Which dog has a famously curled tail?

Which dog is charming and independent?

Did you guess the Shiba Inu?

You are right!

An Ancient Breed

Shiba Inu are often simply called Shibas. Many people believe *Shiba* to mean "brushwood," so some think that these dogs were named for the brushwood bushes where they once hunted. Others believe the name means "small," referring to the dog's size. Although the story of the **breed**'s name is a mystery, what is known is that these dogs date back thousands of years.

More than 14,000 years ago, a group of people called the Jōmon came to Japan. They brought small dogs with them. By 300 BC, more people and their dogs arrived. These dogs bred with **descendants** of the Jōmon people's dogs. This led to new dogs with pointy ears and curly tails.

Japan is an island country in east Asia. Its four main islands are called Hokkaido, Honshu, Kyushu, and Shikoku.
Sea of Japan
Hokkaido
Honshu
Japan
Shikoku
Kyushu
Pacific Ocean

Years later, some of these Japanese dogs were crossed with Chinese and European dogs. Over time, this led to three main kinds of Shiba. Each was named after the region from which it came. Today, there are six distinct Japanese dog breeds, of which Shibas are the smallest.

The first known Shiba to live in the United States arrived in 1954. This dog belonged to an American military family who came over from Japan. However, the breed was not officially recognized by the American Kennel Club (AKC) until 1992. The AKC is an organization that classifies dog breeds by category, based on their heritage and function.

The AKC has a total of seven different groups. Each is made up of dogs with common traits. Shibas are members of the Non-Sporting Group, which includes dogs from a variety of backgrounds. The Chinese Shar-Pei, Lhasa Apso, and Boston terrier are also part of this group.

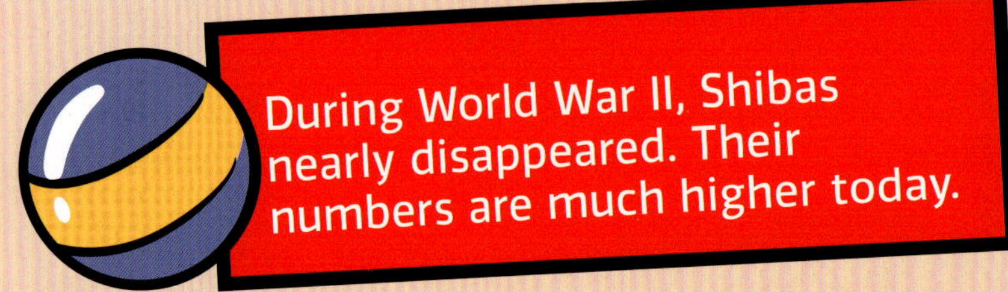

福室有実
朝霞亭

A Shiba's white markings are known as *urajiro*.

Looking Foxy

Shibas are medium-sized dogs. Adult males weigh about 23 pounds (10 kilograms). They stand between 14.5 and 16.5 inches (37 and 42 centimeters) high at the **withers**. Adult females are slightly smaller. They weigh about 17 pounds (8 kg) and are 13.5 to 15.5 inches (34 to 39 cm) high.

Shibas have dense double **coats** of fur. The undercoat is soft, while the outer coat is made of stiff **guard hairs**. This thick coat helps keep Shibas warm and safe. It may be red, cream, red sesame, or black and tan. A Shiba typically has white markings on its face, chest, stomach, legs, and tail. The coloring and features of some Shibas give them a fox-like appearance.

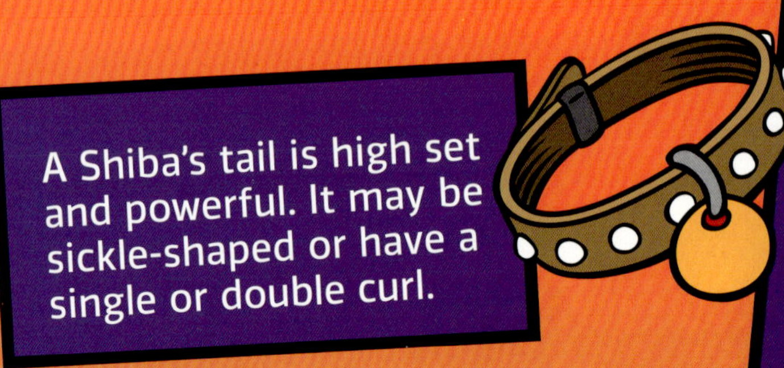

The fur on a Shiba's ears, face, and legs is short. The guard hairs on its body are between 1.5 and 2 inches (4 and 5 cm) long at the withers.

Shibas are compact animals. Their bodies are muscular and sturdy. They have firm backs and well-developed chests. Although their legs are strong, Shibas have a light and smooth stride when they walk.

Shiba Inu have moderately sized heads with flat, broad foreheads. These dogs have dark brown eyes, rimmed with black. They have small ears that tilt forward. Both the eyes and ears of a Shiba Inu are triangular in shape.

Shibas have a black nose and full cheeks. Their muzzle is relatively long, making up about 40 percent of their head length. Shibas have tight black lips and strong jaws. Their teeth are sharp and even.

A Shiba's curled tail may help it avoid losing body heat in cold weather.

The Shiba Personality

Shibas are sometimes described as elegant or dignified. They tend to be courageous and proud. Shibas are also very adaptable. They can feel just as at home in the city as they do in the country.

Most Shibas are fairly quiet. They do not bark much, unless they feel it is absolutely necessary. They are often extremely keen and intelligent. For all of these reasons, many people consider Shibas to be ideal pets.

In Japan, the Shiba Inu's typical personality is described using three words meaning "alertness," "good nature," and "spirited boldness."

Shibas have very high prey drives. They should be leashed when walking to stop them from chasing small animals.

The popularity of Shibas has only increased over time. In 2020, they ranked number 43 on the AKC's list of most popular dog breeds.

However, Shibas are also spirited and can have big personalities. They are often independent, self-confident, and bold. This makes Shibas a charming but challenging breed to handle.

Although they are generally good-natured, Shibas are often **aggressive** around unfamiliar dogs. They can also be **possessive**, especially of their food. It may be a good idea to limit feeding and treats while Shibas are around small children or other dogs.

Shibas usually act reserved or aloof around strangers. However, they are lively and fun around their families. While they may not be the right fit for everyone, Shibas show a great deal of affection and loyalty to people they know well.

Shiba Puppies

The number of puppies in a **litter** depends on the size of the breed. Typically, the smaller the dog, the fewer puppies there are in the litter. Due to their size, Shibas have litters of about two to five puppies. The average litter size is three.

Shibas are a naturally clean breed. They will often groom themselves, much like a cat. This cleanliness makes Shibas easier to housebreak than other breeds. At only four to five weeks old, many Shiba puppies will not leave waste in the same area they sleep. Instead, they will wait to be taken outside.

Between three and seven months of age, a Shiba will typically double in size.

Socialization is necessary for all dog breeds. However, since Shibas can be aggressive toward other dogs, it is even more important for them to be socialized at an early age. Shiba puppies should receive as much socialization training as possible between the ages of two and four months.

Puppies should also be spayed or neutered, depending on their gender. This should be done when they are about four to six months of age. Neutering can be particularly important for male dogs, as it can have a large impact on their temperament. If a male Shiba puppy is neutered at a young age, he may be less aggressive as he grows older.

Supervised interactions with many different people and other dogs are an effective way to help socialize Shibas.

A Shiba's guard hairs repel moisture. This helps to keep the dog warm in winter.

Shibas at Work

Historically, Shibas were bred to be hunting dogs. They have been used to capture a variety of game, both large and small. Their prey typically included rabbits, grouse and other ground birds, wild boar, and other animals. Shibas still retain all of their hunting skills today.

Shibas love being outdoors, even in the snow. In fact, their thick coats allow them to thrive in cold weather. Shibas are also extremely agile and quick. These qualities made them effective hunters, especially in mountainous or forested areas.

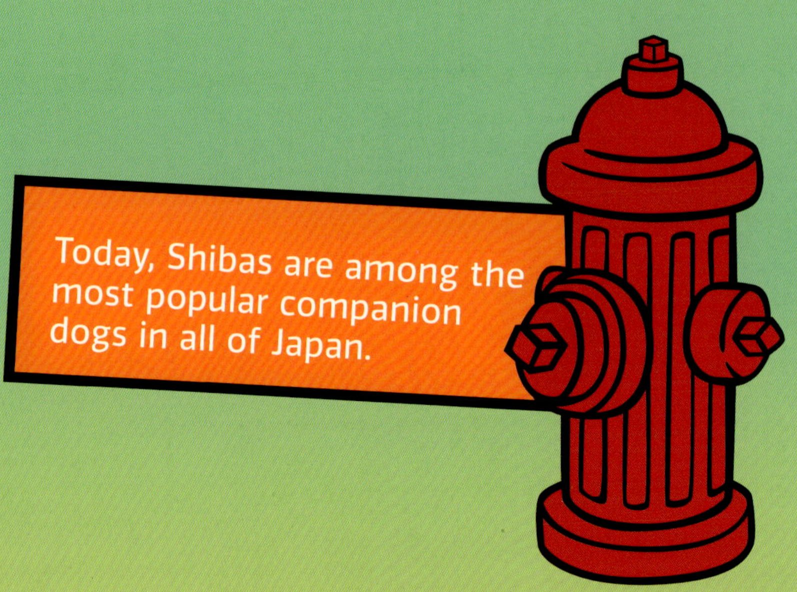

Although hunting was their main job, Shibas have held other positions as well. For instance, some have acted as watchdogs or guard dogs. Their alertness and sharp senses make them well suited for such duties. Other Shibas have served as therapy dogs or service dogs.

Shibas make excellent sporting dogs, too. They may participate in events such as agility or obedience. However, they now primarily work as companion dogs.

In agility events, dogs make their way through a series of obstacles while being guided by their owners.

Because of their strong-willed nature, Shiba Inu are recommended for experienced dog owners.

Caring for a Shiba

Shibas are energetic and active dogs. They need at least one hour of exercise every day. They are always excited to go for a walk with their owners. Playtime can be fun for Shibas, too. They like to chase tennis balls or other fetch toys.

Although they love to be outside, Shibas are notorious escape artists. Shibas should never be left alone outdoors, unless they are in a safe, fully fenced area or other confined space.

Training a Shiba can be hard work. They can be stubborn and strong-willed. However, training can be successful with consistency, creative thinking, and plenty of patience.

Allergies are the most common health issue that Shibas face, though they may not appear until six months of age or later. In most dogs, allergies cause itching or other skin irritations.

Shibas can have knee and hip problems as well. These may be serious health concerns that require surgery to correct. Some Shibas have eye disorders such as cataracts.

Despite these potential problems, Shibas are largely healthy animals. They can bring joy to families for many years. Dog owners must make a lifelong commitment. However, this is especially important with Shibas, since they have a long life expectancy.

Shibas are well known for their heavy shedding. They must be groomed regularly to keep the amount of fur around the house under control.

Shiba Inu Quiz

Q: What job were Shibas originally bred to do?

A: Hunt

Q: What shape are a Shiba's eyes and ears?

A: Triangular

Q: How do Shibas usually act around strangers?

A: Reserved or aloof

Q: Why must Shibas be kept in a fully fenced area?

A: They are notorious escape artists

Q: What country do Shibas come from?

A: Japan

Q: How many puppies are in an average Shiba litter?

A: Three

Key Words

aggressive (uh-GREH-suhv): mean or unfriendly; likely to start a fight

allergies (A-lr-jeez): reactions to particular plants, animals, foods, or other things

breed (BREED): a certain type of animal

coats (KOHTS): the fur of dogs

descendants (duh-SEN-dnts): animals related to another animal that lived in the past

guard hairs (GAARD HEHRZ): long coarse hairs that protect an animal's undercoat

litter (LI-tr): a group of babies born to one animal at the same time

possessive (puh-ZEH-suhv): having a strong desire to keep something for oneself

socialization (so-shuh-lai-ZAY-shn): helping puppies become comfortable around people and other animals in different environments

withers (WI-thrz): the ridge between a four-legged animal's shoulders

Index

Get the best of both worlds.

AV2 bridges the gap between print and digital.

The expandable resources toolbar enables quick access to content including **videos**, **audio**, **activities**, **weblinks**, **slideshows**, **quizzes**, and **key words**.

Animated videos make static images come alive.

Resource icons on each page help readers to further **explore key concepts**.

Published by Lightbox Learning Inc.
276 5th Avenue, Suite 704 #917
New York, NY 10001
Website: www.openlightbox.com

Library of Congress Control Number: 2022933072

ISBN 978-1-7911-4801-0 (hardcover)
ISBN 978-1-7911-4802-7 (softcover)
ISBN 978-1-7911-4327-5 (multi-user eBook)

Printed in Guangzhou, China
1 2 3 4 5 6 7 8 9 0 26 25 24 23 22

022022
101321

Project Coordinator: John Willis
Designer: Terry Paulhus

Photo Credits
Every reasonable effort has been made to trace ownership and to obtain permission to reprint copyright material. The publisher would be pleased to have any errors or omissions brought to its attention so that they may be corrected in subsequent printings. The publisher acknowledges Alamy, Dreamstime, Minden Pictures, Getty Images, and Shutterstock as its primary image suppliers for this title.